BE OUR GHOST

THE FRIGHTENING FLOYDS

Anubis Press
Louisville, KY

Thank you for reading! If you like the book, please leave a review on Amazon and Goodreads. Even if you don't like it, please still leave a review.

To keep up with more Nightmare Press news, join the Anubis Press Dynasty on Facebook.

ANUBIS
PRESS

This one is dedicated to everyone who has supported us. Whether it has been our books, our publishing company, our tours, our pages, at our signings, or even just our posts on social media, we thank you. And to everyone who has approached us in public and spoken to us about our work, we thank you, as well. We wanted to not only bring you some interesting ghost stories and legends about Disney, but a personal glimpse into our lives. Thank you all so much for reading.

BE OUR GHOST

THE FRIGHTENING FLOYDS

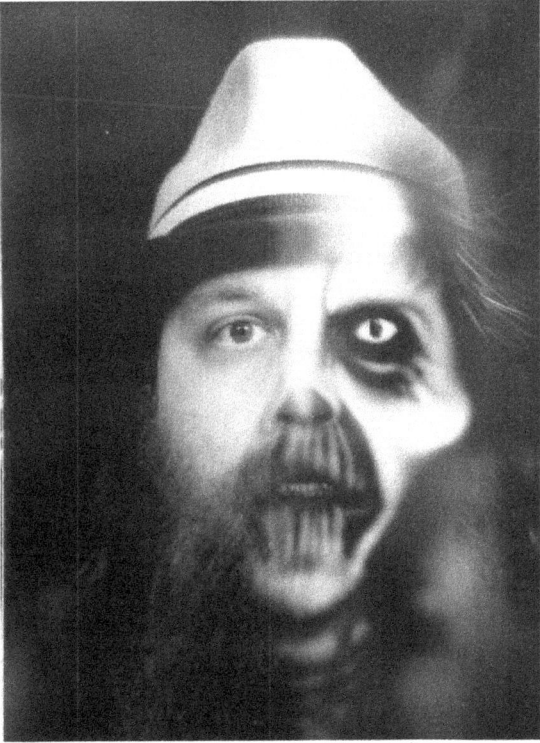
Frightening Floyd Jacob

Frightening Floyd Jenny

TABLE OF CONTENTS

Introduction: A Whole New Spooky World

Good Morning, George…………………………………..01
Disco Debbie and Mr. One Way………………………06
Disney's Haunted Dolls………………………………09
Something Terrifying in the Tower…………………...12
The Ghost Mover………………………………………...17
Cats in the Castle……………………………………...19
Truly Haunted Mansions…………………………....21
Matterhorn Manifestation…………………………36
The Lady on Main……………………………………38
Eerie Epcot……………………………………………39
America Sings…………………………………………57
The Exclusive Club 33…………………………….....58
The Monorail Runner………………………………60
May the Ghosts Be with You………………………62
The Ghost in the Stetson………………………………71
The Urn of Grandma Joyce…………………………79
Peter Pan's Fright………………………………….....80
The Man with No Eyes……………………………...83
Abandoned River Country…………………………..86
Tom Sawyer Island……………………………………89
Walt Still at Disney……………………………………91

Afterword: See You Real Soon……………………...95

The Frightening Floyds' Disney Gallery………………97

About the Authors

Bibliography

INTRODUCTION: A WHOLE NEW SPOOKY WORLD

(Note: This is an unofficial guide and paranormal book about the many Disney parks. Disney has nothing to do with this work.)

Thank you once again for joining us on another haunted excursion. In this book you will read about some of the Disney ghost stories and urban legends coming mostly from Disneyland in Anaheim, California and Walt Disney World in Orlando, Florida, though there are four other Disney theme parks across the globe: Tokyo, Paris, Hong Kong, and Shanghai.

This time we have decided to do something a little different. While we will not go extensively into the backgrounds and histories of these locations, we are going to add a personal touch. As of this writing, the Frightening Floyds have been to Walt Disney World nine times: 2008, 2009, 2010, 2011, 2012, 2014, 2015, 2018, and 2019. We have had some wonderful experiences that created great memories for us. So, in this book we have added a little bit about our visits there.

Though the majority of the ghost stories and little-known facts contained in this work come from online research and YouTube videos, we did unofficially discuss the paranormal claims with some Disney employees during our last two visits to Disney World (2018 and 2019) and a few of them had some very useful information for us. However, as stated above, this is an unofficial work. We did not partner with Disney or any representatives, and no paranormal story within has been confirmed by the Walt Disney Company. We wrote this book as fans of both the paranormal and of Disney.

As we always say, we make no claim to validate, debunk, or otherwise explain these reports. The ghost stories and urban legends are not our experiences but reports made by other individuals. This book is strictly meant to be a fun read for both paranormal fans and Disney enthusiasts. This is not intended to be a reference book. Though the information we gathered from other sources and wrote into this book are true to the best of our knowledge, and though we did extensive research, fact-checking, and cross-referencing, we cannot confirm or deny that any of the history and stories written in here are one-hundred percent accurate. Any misrepresentation or misinterpretation contained herein is not intentional nor of our doing. We have listed all sources in the back. The cast members we talked to wished to remain anonymous, for obvious purposes.

Also, many of the stories are built upon undocumented deaths. Though there have been deaths at the Disney parks, many of the incidents in these ghost stories seem to be myths. Of course, that does not mean that the deaths didn't occur, it just means that it is unlikely that they did. Some of the stories, however, do stem from actual deaths. Neither of these points, we believe, play any part in the validity of the reported ghosts, but we felt this needed to be mentioned nonetheless.

Again, thank you for reading. We hope you enjoy our spooky trip through the happiest place on Earth!

-----The Frightening Floyds

Our first trip to Disney World in 2008. This was Jacob's birthday weekend

Our library is well-stocked with our marvelous first editions — only ghost stories, of course — and photos of your frighteningly friendly ghost writers from the paranormal world. Many stories are ahead, in this second edition of *Be Our Ghost*.

GOOD MORNING GEORGE

Most everyone has heard of the *Pirates of the Caribbean* film franchise, and just about everyone has seen at least one of the movies. Perhaps Johnny Depp's most recognizable role is that of the franchise's main character, Captain Jack Sparrow – an unscrupulous pirate who makes many underhanded moves throughout the films but always seems to come out the hero in the end.

Though the most well known character of the entire series, Depp's stumbling, drunken Keith Richards impersonation isn't the sole reason for the franchise's fame. For more than fifteen years moviegoers have been watching these filthy seafarers sailing across the Caribbean in search of *the Black Pearl*, fleeing Davey Jones, evading the East India Trading Company, escaping ghosts, seeking the Fountain of Youth, or just looking for a good time in Tortuga. This entire sweeping sea epic grew from a simple little Disney ride.

Opened initially in Disneyland on March 18th, 1967, Pirates of the Caribbean was the last attraction that Walt Disney personally worked on. Unfortunately, he did three months before its opening.

Pirates of the Caribbean was originally intended to be a walkthrough wax museum, but was changed to the boat ride concept due to the overwhelming popularity of It's a Small World at the 1964 New York's World Fair. Immense popularity led to the opening of the Disney World attraction at Magic Kingdom in 1973, Tokyo in 1983, Paris in 1992, and Shanghai in 2016.

When we first went to Disney World together in 2008, we arrived at Magic Kingdom when they opened and ran straight for the Pirates ride. We were part of a small crowd doing the same, and many of us stopped to ask a cast member in which direction was the ride. His response was, "I'm not sure. Ask him," and he pointed to a manager who looked both dumbfounded and frightened when the crowd turned his way.

We soon made it to the ride and were pleased to be among the first passengers that day. Before the ride started, the cast members began saying, "Good morning, George" and encouraged the passengers to do the same. We looked at each other and were like, "Who the heck is George?"

It turns out George *was* an Imagineer who worked at Walt Disney World in the 70s. As the story goes, George was a welder who died while working on construction for Pirates of the Caribbean. Speculation as to how he passed has varied. Some say he fell from atop the "Burning City" section of the ride. Others say a large beam fell and crushed him. Another story claims electrocution did him in. The reason the cause of death is not known is there is no official documentation. As far as we can find, no one died during construction of Pirates of the Caribbean. George likely did not even exist, but the story may have come about as a result of two workers who did die there many years later.

Even if there was no George, that doesn't mean there is no spirit. Many visitors have claimed to had strange encounters while on the ride, and they tend to attribute these occurrences to George. Though it is believed that George is a friendly ghost, he does have a tendency to cause disruptions on the ride.

Some workers have reported chilling cold spots near the Burning City. Mysterious footsteps have been heard walking around the ride at night. Others have even claimed to see the ghost of George himself looking down on them from Bombardment Bay. Cast members claim to have seen him walking around building on security cameras. Some who have snapped pictures of themselves or family members while on the ride have captured strange apparitions sitting with them in the boats. While some explain these images away as being mist that is present on many parts of the ride, others say that they truly believe it to be an actual manifestation – most likely of George himself.

Near the scene where the imprisoned pirates are attempting to entice a dog to pass them the keys to their cells, there is a door that somehow comes open on its own. Cast members have found themselves having to close this door repeatedly. They will find it open, close it, and later come back to find it open once again. Most believe George to be the culprit behind these shenanigans, and so the door's unofficial name is "George's Door."

Some believe in the legend so much that they actually say, "Good morning, George," at the start of each day, and "Good night, George" upon leaving for the night. Supposedly, if cast members fail to greet George in the morning, the ride will have problems all day. If they do not bid him farewell at close, the ride will malfunction the following day. Rumor also has it that they might receive mysterious phone calls from the control room late in the night, as well.

We don't exactly know if that's true or not. But when we visited there in 2018, we were among the first guests on the Pirates ride one morning and while Jenny said good morning to the spirit, Jacob did not. The ride did encounter major technical issues, as did several other rides we were on throughout the park that day. Was George letting us know he was not happy that Jacob had forgotten him?

According to some sources, George is not the sole ghost haunting this popular ride. There are allegedly two women whose boat came off the track during the ride's drop and crashed with them in the front, killing them on impact. Supposedly, they still haunt the ride today, making their presences felt as very drastic and sudden drops in temperature and by manifesting on the boat in which they supposedly died. This ghostly duo is known simply as the Ladies. The ride is tame, so it's very difficult to imagine the boats going off track as described. However, anything is possible. Even if the deaths did not occur, that doesn't mean the paranormal reports are necessarily false.

One cast member said she was working the ride and saw two strange-looking women riding in a boat that she had originally thought was empty. The day was slow and there weren't many people on the ride. As the boat was coming, she said she saw two pale females in the boat. It then passed through a dark spot and emerged empty and the women had vanished.

One creepy fact about the Pirates ride in Disneyland is that the skeletons strewn about the various stages were once real human skeletons. It is said that when the ride was first built in 1967, the Imagineers and Walt Disney himself were very disappointed with how unconvincing the fake skeletons were. Former Disney producer, Jason Surrell, reports in his book, *Pirates of the Caribbean: From the Magic Kingdom to the Movies*, Disney obtained authentic human skeletons from the UCLA anatomy department and placed them about the attraction instead.

As technology advanced through the years, faux skeletons began to look much more convincing and the remains scattered across the ride were returned to their respective countries and given proper burials. So, does that mean UCLA knew the skeletons' identities when they let Disneyland use them? Interesting.

Despite the assertion that the skeletons in the ride are now fake, there are some who believe that a few of the real skeletons remain, though they are not sure where, except for one. The rumor is that the skull on the headboard of the bed in the treasure room is still a legitimate human skull. Guests have reportedly asked cast members if this is true, to which the cast members often affirm that it is.

Pirates of the Caribbean is certainly a fun ride, especially if you enjoyed the films. Many aspects from the movies were added over the years, including images of Davey Jones, Blackbeard, and Jack Sparrow himself. In 2017, prior to the release of *Dead Men Tell No Tales,* Depp visited Disneyland in full Jack Sparrow attire and appeared in several locations throughout the attraction.

We definitely enjoy the cool, quiet ride through Disney's dark waters, especially when the day is hot. Not long ago, we watched a YouTube video of the Shanghai version of Pirates and it blew us away. That attraction is a full-blown, CG epic that takes you underwater, through the middle of the sea battles, and even into the ships themselves. We hope to experience this amazing spectacle in person one day. Until then, we are perfectly content with enjoying the Orlando version.

Next time we go, Jacob will be sure to say "Good morning" to George.

Hanging out after the ride. Next time, Jacob will be sure to say
"Good morning" to George

DISCO DEBBIE AND MR. ONE WAY

Space Mountain is a high-speed indoor rollercoaster that sends you hurtling through the dark at about 35-mph. The original in Walt Disney World stands sixty feet tall with a twenty-six foot drop, while the Disneyland version stands seventy feet tall. It is one of Disney's most popular and enduring rides.

The success of Disneyland's Matterhorn Bobsleds inspired Walt Disney to conceptualize the ride, but his death as well as the company's focus on the creation of Walt Disney World in Orlando, Florida led to a postponement in the attraction's development. After Disney World's Magic Kingdom opened to great success, Disney went forward with Space Mountain project and opened it in 1975. The ride became very popular and Disney decided to build a taller version at Disneyland; that version opened in 1977.

Since then, Space Mountain has become a veritable Disney icon. If you visit Magic Kingdom in Disney World, we recommend getting a fast pass for this one because wait times can extend well beyond a couple of hours. If you're anything like us, you won't wait in line anywhere near that long for any ride. One man has allegedly been riding this ride for decades.

Allegedly, not long after the ride opened, a cast member died in the building. Reports of the death are conflicting. One says the man died of an aneurysm behind the building and another says he was a rider who exited the car too early causing an oncoming car to run him down. We're not even sure how the latter is even possible.

Though incidents of death and injury have occurred on Space Mountain in both Disney World and Disneyland, we've found no incidents to match this legend. A woman in her thirties did day on Disneyland's Space Mountain in 1979. After the ride was over, the woman became very ill and could not leave the vehicle. Cast members told her to stay seated while they removed her car from the track. However, this did not happen. The other ride operators were unaware of the situation and the ride started again. The second trip around Space Mountain put the woman in a nearly unconscious state. She later died at the hospital.

In 1983, an 18-year-old man fell off the ride. The injuries sustained in the fall paralyzed him from the waist down. This led to a lawsuit and during the case, the jury had to ride Space Mountain; the court also brought in several of the cars as evidence. In the end, the jury held Disneyland blameless of the accident.

In 1980, a 10-year-old girl passed away of a heart condition after riding Disney World's Space Mountain. The condition was pre-existing and she died due to lack of oxygen.

Another peculiar incident happened in Disney World on Space Mountain in 1998. A falling object struck a man on the head paralyzing his left shoulder and causing short-term memory loss. The memory loss led to his termination from his job. Upon searching the floor of the building, investigators found two objects that could have possibly been the cause: a camera and a candle.

Although no record exists of the red-haired man's alleged death, a combination of these stories may have inspired it. Maybe the legend grew from someone trying to explain the man's ghostly presence.

This man, described as having red hair and a red face, and dressed in 70's era clothing, supposedly haunts the queue. Security cameras have captured his apparition standing on the platform and getting into the cars. Cast members have reported seeing him lingering near the backs of lines.

The spirit is most notorious for getting into cars with single riders. He'll be in the car when the ride starts, but he vanishes before the ride has ended, usually around the final tunnel. This has earned him the nickname, Mr. One Way.

There are other versions of the Mr. One Way story. Some say he doesn't stand around in the queue at all, nor enter the ride behind the rider. Instead, he actually gets into the car from the side where the riders exit.

There is video footage from a Space Mountain security camera floating around YouTube that supposedly captures Mr. One Way entering a car behind a single rider and then sitting next to him. It is certainly an interesting video to watch, but we do not feel it is necessarily ironclad paranormal evidence. If you watch closely, you can see the alleged Mr. One Way moves in tandem with the rider and looks very similar to him, so it may actually just be a double exposure of the rider. Granted, we do not necessarily believe this is the definitive explanation, but it's very possible this was not Mr. One Way.

That also doesn't mean that this explanation for this one incident necessarily debunks the existence of Mr. One Way. Many people have seen him, and there are even reports of him hanging out in the cast member locker rooms. His apparition is often seen standing about and moving across the rooms. Hard to call that double exposure.

Another version of the Mr. One Way story alleges that the specter in question is actually a young boy who died mysteriously on the ride. Some say that the while the adult version does not interact with guests, the young boy will, often looking at them and even talking to them. Is this a case of one story altering as it is told, or are there actually two one-way ghosts?

These two spirits are not alone on Space Mountain. There is the glowing ghost of a young woman who was supposed to have once been a cast member who also died of an aneurysm behind the building (coincidence?). People have seen her ghost appear emitting a phosphorescent glow while flying around different areas of the ride. Reports claim that she hovers in the darkness throughout the building. Others claimed to have spotted her in the old Starfield window in the indoor waiting area. Due to her glowing nature, she has been dubbed Disco Debbie. But our question is this: Is the green flying form actually the ghost of a former cast member, or is it merely Tinkerbell?

On a non-paranormal-but-still-very-creepy note: There is an urban legend of an Imagineer standing up on the ride too soon while testing it and being decapitated as a result. No record of this exists, but some believe it to have actually happened. Could that actually be Mr., One Way?

Of course, a premature death is never a laughing matter. But the deaths in the ghost stories are speculative. However, that does not mean that spirits of past workers or guests could not dwell there at Space Mountain. It is, after all, the Ghosts Galaxy.

THE FRIGHTENING FLOYDS

DISNEY'S HAUNTED DOLLS

For many years, It's a Small World has been one of Disney's most famous (and infamous) rides. Located in the Fantasyland section of most Disney parks, It's a Small World is meant to promote the idea of global unity and harmony. It is a water-based dark ride that rolls lazily through various stages that represent the different nations of the world. The entire ride consists of mechanical childlike puppets continuously singing the title song. The attraction debuted at the 1964 New York World's Fair before becoming a permanent fixture at Disneyland in 1965.

Despite being about unity and togetherness, this ride has creeped out many people through the years. Many folks have found the repetition of the song and the dolls themselves to be rather unsettling. There have been stories of people going into near panic attacks while on this ride. We do have to say that when we rode it, we did find it to be a little spooky. Something just seems disturbingly bizarre about the entire attraction. But, we didn't see any ghosts.

But others have.

According to legend, there were cast members who loved the ride so much that their spirits came back to it in the afterlife. In the Disneyland version of the attraction, lights will turn off and on by themselves, as will the dolls. After the park is closed and the ride shut down, employees have reported puppets still signing and moving. Others state to have walked past some puppets only to have their heads turn or their eyes follow their movements. There have been other reports claiming that puppets disappear from one spot and reappear in another. Some vanish altogether. Cast members believe that the ghosts of the past employees are inside the puppets, making them sing and move.

Most likely, the puppets that keep moving even after the electricity is off are just malfunctioning. Regardless, one can see how it might be disturbing if the electronic dolls are active without electricity. They are disturbing enough when the ride is operational. Could it really be that something supernatural keeps them moving even when the ride is off?

Moving among the puppets of It's a Small World

SOMETHING TERRIFYING IN THE TOWER

One of Jacob's favorite rides at Walt Disney World is Hollywood's Tower of Terror, but not so much one of Jenny's. In fact, the last time they visited Hollywood Studios, Jacob had to ride it by himself.

On the ride, you sit with others in a faux elevator as it rises towards the top of the tower, which stands an impressive 199 feet tall, and then it falls rapidly, rises again, and then falls once more—or, at least that's the effect. In truth, the 'plummet' isn't actually a fall but a pull. During the drop, the pulley system pulls the elevator fast enough to create the illusion that it is falling. So, the "fall" isn't really a fall and is actually very secure. However, you do not want to forget your seatbelts on this one since it is an intense drop sensation.

Another interesting fact about the Tower of Terror is that the computer system operating the ride runs a random drop sequence, which means that the number of drops riders experience varies with each run. That explains why one time when Jacob rode it he wondered if the ride was broken because it kept rising and falling repeatedly as if it was never going to stop. It rose and "fell" a lot more than it had the first time he'd rode it.

The theme for the Tower of Terror as of this writing is *The Twilight Zone*, one of Jacob's all-time favorite shows, so he was attracted to the ride from the start. Upon developing the ride, Imagineers reportedly watched 156 episodes of the classic television show in preparation. However, *The Twilight Zone* was not the original concept Disney planned to use. They had kicked around several haunted attraction ideas beforehand, such as a ride based on Stephen King's novels, a whodunit murder mystery, a ride narrated by Mel Brooks, and a Vincent Price ghost tour.

Guardians of the Galaxy replaced *The Twilight Zone* theme at the Disneyland version, which is understandable considering that

Guardians is a Disney product and not nearly as dated as *The Twilight Zone,* but Jacob has his fingers crossed that the attraction in Disney World never changes. While he does like *Guardians of the Galaxy*, it doesn't come close to equaling his love for *The Twilight Zone.*

Moving on to the beyond, let us tell you about the spirit reported to haunt the tower. Rumor has it that there are a few ghosts lingering around the attraction, but the most well known is the bellhop who is said to have died there long ago.

As the story goes, on Platform D, one of the cast members dropped dead from a heart attack while loading passengers. At the close of each day, the bellhops have to check that the ride is working properly. Those who have gotten Platform D have had terrifying ghostly experiences while doing so. The ride sometimes freezes, lights turn off and on along the corridors, and the holographic ghosts won't work on cue, a few of them sometimes appearing in areas that are not their designated spots.

There have also been reports of a ghostly bellhop appearing in the Boiler Room just before you board the ride. Some have described seeing him out of the corner of their eyes but not being able to see him once they look in his direction. A former cast member there reports to have seen a bellhop she did not recognize in the area. When she went to speak to him, he went into a dark corner and disappeared. Others have claimed to see an unknown bellhop standing still, not paying attention to anyone, and then being gone when they look back at him once again.

A video surfaced on YouTube some time back of a maintenance person testing the ride. In the video, you can see different transparent images of another man sitting behind and beside the worker. It is clear and unmistakable that it is the image of another human being (or former human being), but while some believe this to be the infamous bellhop ghost, others say it is simply past security footage overlapping with the current.

This explanation makes sense considering the "ghost" is clearly not dressed as a bellhop and looks to have on a button-up work shirt open at the collar. However, that's not to say that it could not be spectral. The ghost rider might very well not be a worker and just be wearing a button-up shirt. Maybe he isn't the bellhop but a past guest who somehow returned. When you consider the number of ghostly reports coming from workers and guests on the ride, it is a claim that certainly warrants consideration.

Whether or not you visit the Tower of Terror, looking for ghosts (real ones) or you're just there to enjoy the ride, maybe keep an eye out for any paranormal passengers or spirits wandering the halls.

Our first time riding Tower of Terror in 2009. We are on the bottom left.

This picture is from 2015. Look to the far right of the middle row. Notice how Jenny is not present in this one. Jacob knew where the cameras were.

THE FRIGHTENING FLOYDS

THE GHOST MOVER

The original PeopleMover ride opened in Disneyland's Tomorrowland on July 2nd, 1967. The ride consists of small train cars on an elevated track moving in a circular path around the park. The trains stayed in constant motion, so upon boarding, the passengers would have to catch a car and hop in. Each train consisted of four cars colored red, yellow, blue, or green. They were repainted white with colored stripes in 1987. Amid budget cuts, the ride shut down in August of 1995 for being outdated.

Though hardly a thrill ride, a few tragic accidents did occur on it. Only about a month after being open, a young man jumping between cars fell on the tracks as the ride entered a tunnel, causing another train to crush him.

In 1972, a teenage girl lost her mouse cap while on the ride and she and a friend jumped onto the track to retrieve it. The friend made it safely into another car but the girl ran through a tunnel and out an exit door. The exit led to a thirty-foot drop to the concrete below; she broke her arm, hip, and pelvis, forcing her into a body brace.

In June of 1980, an eighteen-year-old man found himself caught between cars as the ride entered the SuperSpeed Tunnel. After getting out of his seat and trying to move to another car, he became pinned between them. Unable to escape, the two cars then crushed him to death.

Despite the ride shutting down in 1995, the ghost of one of the young men killed on the ride allegedly haunts the park. In the Tomorrowland ExpoCenter, located where the PeopleMover once was, the ghost will often pull blond women's hair. One cast member said she's had her hair pulled by someone unseen several times in that building. She says that another cast member sees the ghost walking through the building quite often. She has felt someone pulling on her hair only to turn and see the boy's ghostly image walking several feet away from her. When she follows him, he'll turn a corner and vanish. Both of these cast members are blond.

The ride's popularity in California led to the opening of a PeopleMover in Walt Disney World in 1975. This one is still operational. We thoroughly enjoy the ride through the sky. It's a nice place to rest, catch a breeze, and see all the activity in the Magic Kingdom. We're certainly not the only ones. There is always a long line waiting to board.

CATS IN THE CASTLE

An interesting and little-known secret about Disneyland regards the feral cats that roam the park at night. In 1955, when Walt wanted to put an attraction inside of Sleeping Beauty Castle, he and the Imagineers entered to find that many stray cats had made the castle their home, bringing with them a mighty flea infestation.

Before Disney could create the Walkthrough Attraction, they needed to find a solution to the feline crowding. They knew they couldn't outright eliminate the animals, as that would no doubt bring them some very bad publicity. Instead, they adopted the cats out to other cast members to ensure each animal would have a good home.

Soon after fixing the feline problem, imagineers discovered that the park had attracted quite the rodent population. Mice other than Mickey and Minnie were now running rampant across Disneyland. Lucky for Disney, they didn't find all of the cats a permanent home. Many cats hadn't made their home in Sleeping Beauty Castle, probably because there was too much good hunting in the rural area around the park.

Disney then decided to allow the cats to continue hunting through the parks. They set up feeding stations around Disneyland, spayed and neutered all the cats, and provided them medical care when needed.

Most often, these cats come out at night. However, some wander into the daylight and sleep in various places around Disneyland. The most common areas to find them are along the tracks by Main Street, White Water Snacks, and the cliffs of Big Thunder Rail. Guests are not encouraged to engage the animals since they are strays. In fact, Disney doesn't want the public to be aware of the secret cat colony. They managed to keep it concealed until there was an article published about it in the *Los Angeles*

Times in 2010. This resulted in a lot of positive feedback from animal rights groups, but Disney was reportedly not too happy about all the attention the article received. Now the legend is well known and the cats of Disneyland even have their own Facebook page.

To this day, an estimated two-hundred cats remain on property. If any of them become too comfortable being around humans, Disney adopts them out to cast members. The cat might be out of the bag about this arrangement, but Disney still wants to keep their furry pest control team as isolated from the guests as possible.

TRULY HAUNTED MANSIONS

One of Disney's most famous attractions is the Haunted Mansion. Located at nearly every Disney theme park around the world, this ride has entertained guests for decades. The first version opened at Disneyland back in 1969; the second came to Disney World's Magic Kingdom in 1971; Tokyo Disneyland opened theirs in 1983. The Haunted Mansion was also the inspiration for Phantom Manor in Disney Paris and Hong Kong's Mystic Manor, which is more fantasy themed and does not refer to ghosts.

As you might know by now, we are quite the fans of anything haunted, whether as a fictitious attraction or an allegedly real haunted location. Haunted Mansions is one of our favorite rides in all of Disney. It really brings out the enjoyable aspects of a good ghostly location. Even waiting to get on the ride is fun. As you near the entrance doors, you will come upon a faux graveyard that has humorous one-liners etched upon the tombstones. If you pay attention, you can even find the fortuneteller Madam Leota's resting site. On the way out, you will find a pet cemetery with more tongue-in-cheek writings upon the gravestones. In the Disney World location, you'll find a small memorial statue of Mr. Toad from *the Wind in the Willows.* This is but one of the hidden Mr. Toads around the park, as Mr. Toad's Wild Ride was once an attraction in the Orlando park, but was replaced by the Many Adventures of Winnie the Pooh in 1998. The ride still exists at Disneyland and has ever since the day the park first opened. When riding the Pooh ride in 2018, Jacob managed to spot the hidden picture of Mr. Toad on the wall just as you entered one of the rooms.

The Haunted Mansion is a dark ride that is good to rest and cool down on. As your "Doom Buggy" makes its way through the specter-filled shadows, you will see a number of different frights waiting in the darkness. You'll see hitchhiking ghosts, the ghostly head of fortuneteller Madam Leota, and a ballroom full of dancing spirits. But these props and holograms don't seem to be the only ghosts in the mansion. There have been reports of real phantoms lingering in the halls, seats, and shadows.

One of those ghosts is the Man with the Cane. This cane-carrying entity rides the attraction late at night, sitting silently by himself in one of the Doom Buggies. He always sits still, staring straight ahead, and acknowledging nothing around him. Cast members have tried to speak to him but he never responds. Witnesses report that he vanishes before the ride ends. There have even been incidents where employees closing down the ride have heard the click-clack tapping of a cane echoing somewhere in the darkness. This sound very well could be some mechanism on the ride, an animal, or something settling in the building, but it has chilled some of those who have heard it.

It is not clear who this man is, but some think he may be the spirit of a pilot who supposedly died in a plane crash back in the 40s. This plane allegedly crashed where Bay Lake Tower now stands. Of course, there was no Walt Disney World back then, but those who tell the tale believe that the pilot has decided to hang around Disney World, particularly the Haunted Mansion. We're not sure why the pilot would have a cane, though. We can't imagine the plane crash caused him to carry a limp into the afterlife.

We could not find any evidence that this tragic event even happened. However, that does not mean that it didn't, though it does seem likely that there would be some article about it if it had. Even if the crash is nothing but a legend, that still does not mean that the Man with the Cane's ghost doesn't haunt the halls, he just might be someone else.

The ghost of a young boy also reportedly haunts the Walt Disney World Haunted Mansion. A while back, a picture surfaced on the internet of a young boy peeking out from his Doom Buggy at the people behind him. The photographer just happened to be snapping a picture and caught the kid on camera. This person says that there were no children this age anywhere within twenty people of them in line; and they pose the question as to why this child was looking back in their direction.

It can certainly have been just a child turning in his seat to look behind him for some unknown reason. It would be hard to say with certainty no children of this age were around you in such a large crowd. It does look rather odd, however. The Doom Buggies are spacious and this child seems to be leaning very far out, which would be difficult since there are safety bars on the ride to deter this sort of action. So it is an interesting picture.

That's not the only little boy said to haunt one of the Haunted Mansions. In Disneyland, a mother spread her seven-year-old son's ashes on the Haunted Mansion because it was his favorite ride. When the staff noticed her doing it, they stopped the ride and commenced a cleanup of the ashes. Though they worked diligently to sweep it all up, it seems as though they were unable to get it all, for now the spirit of the boy supposedly remains behind.

The story goes that the boy can be heard crying for his mother at the end of the ride, and at night when the ride is shut down. Some guests have reported seeing a little boy sitting alone in a Doom Buggy, only to not be there the next time they look. Cast members have seen the little boy crying by the exit, and when they ask him what's wrong, he ignores them and disappears.

At close, there have been times when the workers waiting around to make sure no one else sneaks onto the ride have heard a little boy's laughter in the hallways. Cast members have mistaken this for the approach of a family coming for the ride. As they wait for the group's approach, ready to explain to them that the ride is shutting down, no one ever comes.

Strange movements supposedly occur in the shadows and in the employees' periphery, but no ghost is ever seen. Others complain of mysterious chills when this occurs. One cast member who experienced this said that as she stood there waiting for whoever was laughing to arrive, she felt the sudden onset of chills and then a hand touched her back. Startled, she spun around only to find that she was alone in the dark,

No Disney parks allow remains to be scattered but there are several urban legends that this has happened at many of the parks. Several of these stories claim the scattering has led to the presence of spirits as well.

There is an urban legend about a woman who reviewed the Disneyland version of the ride before it opened in 1969 and found it so scary that she died of a heart attack. We don't know if this claim has any validity to it or not. Because of this supposed death, the woman allegedly haunts the ride. Cast members have reported seeing a strange woman wandering the darkened halls where no one should be walking. When they call after her, she disappears.

After the ride closes at night, employees can sometimes hear her haunting screams ringing through the dark. Upon checking security cameras and physically investigating the area, no one is ever there. Guests have also claimed to see the woman riding the ride alone, only to see her Doom Buggy is empty the next time they look.

Another incident that happened before the ride's opening was that of strange music playing in the Séance Room. A worker was making rounds of the building and heard the music so clearly that he believed a radio was inside the wall. After listening for a little while, he noticed commercials or a DJ never interrupted the music, nor was it recognizable as any sort of popular music that would normally play on the radio. Keep in mind this was in the 1960s before tape recorders were common. The strange and unidentifiable music continued for days until the workers decided to install speakers to drown out the music. As far as we know, the source of the music was never determined and there haven't been any further reports regarding it.

The ghosts of the Haunted Mansion are worldwide. It seems that Tokyo Disneyland's version of the Haunted Mansion has its own resident specter. One man, when asked what he thought of the ride, said that the "unmoving woman at the end of the hallway was certainly the scariest". As it turns out, there is no such woman at the end of the hallway. Other guests have reported seeing her as well.

Some other interesting, non-paranormal facts about the Haunted Mansion:

The character of Madam Leota—the fortuneteller in the Séance Room—was named and modeled after the Imagineer who built her. Fittingly enough, the Imagineer's name was Leota Toombs. On the night of her daughter's school dance—the daughter who would also become an Imagineer (Kim Irvine)—Leota rehearsed her incantations. This allegedly freaked Kim's date out and he asked, "Wow, what's up with your mom?" After Leota Toombs passed,

Disney had Kim film some new Madam Leota footage. While Leota Toombs was the face of Madame Leota, Eleanor Audley provided the voice. Audley played the voice of Maleficent in the 1959 Disney classic, *Sleeping Beauty.*

That's not all there is about the Séance Room. According to legend, the table in the room is extremely old and was used in actual séances, purchased from people alleged to be seers. The book that once sat upon the table in Disney World was supposedly a 14th-century witchcraft book somehow obtained from an alleged witch. Legend has it that the book would move around on its own. Cast members could not keep it in the upright position and often times they couldn't even keep it in the correct spot on the table.

Former Imagineer, Yale Gracey, inspired *The Haunted Mansion* film's character, Master Gracey. Gracey was a master of illusion and considered by fans and cast members alike to be the unofficial lord of the manor at the Haunted Mansion.

We had an interesting experience on the ride once. On the very same day that Jacob neglected to tell George "Good morning", the Haunted Mansion kept breaking down. While we were on the ride, it must have stopped two or three times. Once, it stopped right in front of the singing statue quartet and we had to listen to them sing for several minutes.

An interesting fact about those statues is that the baritone singer among them is none other than Thurl Ravenscroft. If that name doesn't ring a bell, perhaps the name of one of the characters he voiced will: Tony the Tiger, the Frosted Flakes mascot that says, "They're grrrreat!" Ravenscroft also sang, "You're a Mean One, Mr. Grinch" from the classic Christmas cartoon, *How the Grinch Stole Christmas.*

Towards the end of the ballroom scene at Disneyland's Haunted Mansion, you will see two portraits of men shooting at each other. One of these portraits has a real bullet hole in it. As the story goes, in the summer of 1974, a guest took out a gun and shot at the portrait, putting a hole in the glass. Some say the gun went off accidentally. Imagineers have since covered the hole with a spider.

Regarding that spider, there are a few other stories as to why it is there. One story says that a child brought a rock with him on the ride to protect him from ghosts, and when he thought one of the spirits got too close, he threw the rock at it and hit the portrait.

Another simply states that the spider was one of many excess creatures created for the ride and was used about two years after the attraction's opening to cover an empty space. Another rumor is that employees originally placed the spider in that spot during the first year the mansion adopted the *Nightmare before Christmas* theme at holiday time. At that time, the spider was green and red to match the festivities. When Christmas passed, the Imagineers tried to remove the spider but found they had secured it in so tightly that it could not be undone. Since they couldn't remove the spider, they painted it black and purple and left it. Each of these accounts ends with Imagineers in Florida placing a spider in the same spot simply for the sake of symmetry between the parks.

Those are just some fun facts, urban legends, and ghost stories about the Haunted Mansion. As previously stated, it has always been one of our favorite attractions. When we went to Disney World in 2018, we brought our book, *Kentucky's Haunted Mansions,* to the Magic Kingdom with us for the sole purpose of taking our picture with it in front of the mansion. While there, one of the cast members nearby gave us some pointers on a good shot and helped us set the picture up. As always, the workers there are very kind and helpful. That's part of what makes Disney World such a great place to visit.

One side of the Haunted Mansion from the queue

The old-fashioned ghost hearse in front of the Haunted Mansion.
Where is the horse?

The grave of Madame Leota

The anteroom of the Mansion; the ceiling rises to reveal the rest of the portraits underneath

The signing statues

The pet cemetery outside of the Haunted Mansion

The Mr. Toad memorial statue

Jenny surviving the Haunted Mansion

Jacob barely made it out alive

BE OUR GHOST

MATTERHORN MANIFESTATION

The Matterhorn in the Fantasyland area of Disneyland was the first steel roller coaster in the world when it opened alongside the Disneyland Monorail and Submarine Voyage in June of 1959. Together, these three openings were part of the Tomorrowland expansion. The ride officially became part of Fantasyland in 1970. The company drew inspiration for the ride from the Matterhorn in the Alps.

In 1978, it underwent its first renovations, which changed the trains and added more themes in the tunnels, and added the Abominable Snowman. Over the last decade, it has experienced many refurbishments as age has worn it down.

The Matterhorn's claim to fame rests with being the world's first steel roller coaster. Its claim to infamy, however, is in the two deaths that occurred on it. The first happened in 1964 and was the park's first fatality. A fifteen-year-old boy stood up and fell out after his ride companion had reportedly undone his seatbelt. He died three days later from the injuries sustained in the fall.

The second death is the best known. On January 3rd, 1984, 48-year-old Regena "Dolly" Young was decapitated by another bobsled after being thrown from hers. An investigation into the cause of her fall showed that her safety belt had been unbuckled, but since she had ridden alone, it could not be determined whether she did this herself or if the belt was faulty. Since this tragedy, park employees who have worked the Matterhorn call the area "Dolly's Dip" and believe Dolly's lingering spirit haunts there.

Staff members claim to see her sometimes riding the ride and lingering on the tracks. Supposedly, late at night, they have heard her scream near the spot where she fell. One former park employee said she hated walking the tracks after the ride closed because she always felt a supernatural presence watching her. This feeling became so oppressive that she dreaded every time she had to walk it.

If these accounts are accurate, we wonder if Dolly does indeed haunt the Matterhorn or is it just residual energy remaining from her premature death.

BE OUR GHOST

THE LADY ON MAIN

Y ou can't research too many ghost stories and/or urban legends without finding one about a woman in a white, grey, blue, or black dress. Disney is no different. They have a ghost called the Woman in White. This ghost appears on Disneyland's Main Street, U.S.A, for which Walt's childhood hometown of Kansas City, MO provided inspiration, as did the Henry Ford Museum & Greenfield Village. The street is supposed to represent an average turn-of-the-century American town.

When visible, the woman that allegedly haunts the street is easy to notice; she is said to be pale and wearing a white, Victorian-era dress. Those who have seen her say she is friendly, often times smiling at them as she passes. Some have been briefly taken aback by her peculiar and out-of-place appearance, and when they turn back to get another look at her, she is gone.

Her identity is unknown, but the cast members who have seen her believe her to be someone who passed away on the premises long before Disneyland ever existed. We feel that this is a no-brainer considering her attire. Disneyland was certainly not around in the Victorian era. But whoever she is, she spends her time in limbo doing a good deed by leading lost children to the Disneyland Baby Care Center so they are able to locate their parents. A few lost children who have found their way to the center have said a woman in a white dress led them there. Some speculate that the old time atmosphere of Main Street is what attracted her.

Who the lady on Main Street is, she is most certainly seems to be a good spirit.

EERIE EPCOT

Opened in 1982, Disney's Epcot was Walt Disney World's second theme park. Predicated upon an idea Walt called the Experimental Prototype Community of Tomorrow, Epcot's initial intention was to be the ceaseless blueprint of tomorrow's living. It was also the original concept for the entire property that became Walt Disney World, but the ambitious project was unrealized. Epcot is a small portion of that realization, as the park's theme is the celebration of technological innovation and international cultures.

The park's divided into two major sections: Future World, which hosts numerous pavilions that explore technological advancements and innovations; the other area is the World Showcase, which has eleven pavilions dedicated to the cultures of specific countries. The eclectic blend of current culture and futuristic progress is why Epcot has been called the "permanent world's fair".

Though Epcot is very much rooted in the future, there are pieces of the past apparently still hanging on.

Located at the center of the park is Spaceship Earth, the massive geodesic sphere that is the symbol of the entire park. It's a fifteen-minute dark ride that takes passengers back in time to chronicle the evolution of man beginning in prehistoric times and going into visions of the future. It also contains an interactive aspect that allows you to determine what your ideal future home would look like. It's a fun attraction and we make sure to ride it each time we visit Epcot.

According to legend, a couple of people enjoyed the ride so much that they just couldn't leave it. Guests and staff alike have reported spotting ghostly children on the ride. A boy and a blond girl with long hair reportedly ride in cars together - cars that were empty when the ride started. When the ride ends, they are no longer there. They have also been seen running and playing in the boarding area, as well as around where passengers disembark. Some have even said the children vanished right in front of them.

One cast member told a story about a guest coming to them and telling them of two kids, a girl and boy, who were without their parents getting on the ride. The guest said she noticed the two kids all by themselves get into the car in front of her, and later in the ride, she noticed they weren't there. After checking the ride and the cameras, employees found no children matching those descriptions.

In Epcot's France pavilion, there is Impressions de France, a film that gives the viewers a cultural tour of France and its many regions. The film runs about eighteen minutes and is projected upon five adjacent screens, giving it 200-degree coverage, and is very similar to a Cinerama screen. Impressions de France has been running since the day Epcot opened and holds the Guinness World Record for the "longest running daily screening of a film in the same theater".

There are stories about a strange man who won't leave the theater after close. When employees approach him to escort him out, he is no longer there when they reach his seat.

One employee said this has happened numerous times to a few different cast members. She said she never experienced it personally, but she did hear someone talking in the waiting area, very distinctly, and when she went in there, no one was present. She thought the last of the guests had left several minutes before, so it struck her as rather odd. She then found a co-worker and asked him if he had been talking, and he replied that he hadn't. They looked around the building and found no one else. Could it have been the ghost from the theater or just a straggler hanging around after close?

Epcot has many fascinating attractions, from rides to educational films. We've not seen the ghosts, but we have certainly enjoyed the many rides and features of the World Showcase. We visited Epcot once and spent eight hours just wandering the pavilions of each country. Before they opened the Coca-Cola bar in Disney Springs, we made sure to visit Club Cool, a little stop in Epcot where you can sample different flavors of Coke from around the world.

One time, when we visited in summer, it was an excruciatingly hot day, and a sudden storm blew in. As it neared, we were walking past the large fountains at the front of the park and the wind was blowing the water over onto us. Between the cool breeze, the light wind, and the mist coming at us from the fountain, it was a nice moment to cool down. This has always been one of our favorite memories.

We haven't gone to Impressions de France, yet. Maybe we'll check it out on our next visit and maybe see a little something extra if we are there late at night.

At the Epcot International Flower & Garden Festival in 2009

The Seas with Nemo and Friends

Having fun at Epcot

At Epcot before the rope drops – 2019

By the Dia de Muertos statues inside the Mexico pavilion

Still in Mexico!

Troll at the Norway pavilion

Hanging out in Norway – 2019

Meeting Elsa at Norway

Meeting Ana in Norway

Jacob with his Epcot shirt at Epcot

Taking selfies around the world!

Hello?

The many wonders of Epcot

The Beyond Burger at Liberty Inn in the American pavilion

THE FRIGHTENING FLOYDS

AMERICA SINGS

In 1974, tragedy struck Disneyland. Located in the round building that recently held Innoventions and Super Hero HQ, and had previously housed the Carousel of Progress at the park's eastern end, was an attraction in its opening year called America Sings. This attraction featured audio animatronics that sang songs from different periods in US history. The ride was held in a rotating theater, and this rotation resulted in a harrowing event that transpired only two weeks after the opening.

At the time, 18-year-old Debbie Stone was a cast member working the ride. On the evening of July 8th, while the attraction was in motion, Debbie, who had been standing in an area between the rotating audience section and the stationary stage wall, was caught between the two and crushed to death. This account is factual, and not one of the urban legends. Because of this horrible incident, the stationary walls were replaced with breakaway walls, and a safety light was installed in order to let the operator know if someone had gotten too close to the walls.

According to legend, Debbie has remained at Disneyland. In an effort to keep people from suffering the same fate as she did, people claim they can hear her say, "Be careful" whenever anyone gets too close to the walls. Some reports allege that at night, when the park is closed and the ride shut down, the echo of Debbie's final screams can be heard. Cast members have also reported feeling cold spots where Debbie died, and some have even claimed to see Debbie's transparent form standing by the wall.

Skeptics believe that the claim about hearing her spirit warn others away from the wall was invented to give Debbie's end some meaning. Naturally, others think her ghost could very well still be there, watching the area in which she spent her final moments. Perhaps her residual energy remains and that is what people are experiencing. Or, perhaps it's nothing more than Disney lore.

THE EXCLUSIVE CLUB 33

Anyone who follows Disney much, or enjoys conspiracy theories, has most likely heard all the theories regarding Disney and their supposed goal of global domination. At the center of these perceived cloak and dagger operations is Club 33 – the most exclusive organization within Disney.

As Walt Disney was attempting to gain backing from major corporations for his many projects, he made connections with some very powerful individuals, with Ford, General Electric, and Pepsi-Cola being among the first to get on board with his vision. He had approached these companies at the 1964 World's Fair in New York and made a good impression.

While seeking aid from these massive corporations, Walt found himself in the luxurious VIP lounges occupied by the men who ran them. This, in turn, made an impression on him. The idea of having a private place to entertain guests remained in the back of his mind as Disneyland was in development.

After the park opened, Walt invited these men to Disneyland to see what they helped create. When Walt told General Electric his ideas for the Carousel of Progress, they were solidly behind it, but they wanted him to install a VIP lounge for them by the attraction. He told them that there wasn't room for such a place near the ride, but that he had just the place elsewhere to put this lounge. Thus, Club 33 opened at 33 Royal Street, New Orleans Square.

This location is for the rich and powerful sponsors and visitors to Disneyland to unwind. However, some believe this secret club to be an illicit and shadowy organization that devises schemes to take over the world.

With the club remaining under such a shroud of mystery, and with the costs for joining being allegedly between $25k and $50k, with anywhere from $10k to $30k supposedly being an annual fee, the rumors only seem more likely to some. The club limits the number of members to a hundred, which has created a ten-year waiting list.

Disney has been the subject of many illuminati conspiracy theories. Who can forget the alleged subliminal messages hidden in their movies? But what makes Club 33 so curious to some is the usage of the number 33. Why 33? Well, some say the number comes from the club's address. Another theory is that the number represents Disney's 33 sponsors at the time the club opened. The conspiracy theorists have another answer.

In Freemasonry, once someone achieves the level of Master Mason, he is able to extend his learning of the Scottish Rite by taking further degrees; thirty-three is the highest degree. Conspiracy theorists have long said Walt Disney was a freemason and illuminati member. This only gives further weight to the suspicions for those who believe it.

There have been lawsuits recently filed by members who were banned from Club 33 for reasons they believed were unjust. These suits have helped bring to light some of what goes on behind the closed doors. The suits don't seem to have done too much damage. Club 33 is now open at Walt Disney World.

While those who are not members, or know members, may never actually know what is going on in the club, it's probably safe to say that Disney is merely going for privacy and not up to any wicked rituals or iniquitous subterfuge.

BE OUR GHOST

THE MONORAIL RUNNER

The Disneyland Monorail System has always been one of Disney's most unique and recognizable innovations. When it opened in June 1959, it was the first monorail system to operate daily in the western hemisphere. It came at a time when America was experiencing a growing obsession with automobiles, and Walt wanted to build on that and create what he envisioned as a means of transportation for the future. The taller and faster Walt Disney World monorail opened in 1971. This highway in the sky has been transporting Disney-goers for more than half a century now.

Even though it's a well-loved and often-used Disneyland attraction, it does have its dark side. It is also the location of a Disney phantom known as the Grad Night Ghost. Every June, Disneyland stays open all night for Grad students, and in 1966, one student met his end there.

Nineteen-year-old Thomas Guy Cleveland scaled one of Disneyland's perimeter fences and climbed up onto the monorail, trying to sneak into the park. A security guard spotted him walking along the track and yelled for him to get down. Thomas fled the other way down the track. Seconds later, the monorail came barreling along at about 40 miles-per-hour and slammed into him, dragging him about 30 or 40 feet to his death. This is a true and documented death.

Now, ever since Thomas's fateful night, he has remained atop those tracks, running from the monorail as it passes. Folks on the ground have looked up and thought they saw someone running, only to look again and not see him. Monorail drivers have reported seeing Thomas's frightening apparition coming towards them on the tracks at the end of the park where he died, but he disappears before they run him down. It seems that Thomas's ghost only appears at night.

The monorails are metal trains weighing several tons, and they move down those tracks at thirty-plus miles per hour. The rails are forty feet in the air, higher in Disney World. Climbing upon on them will almost certainly result in serious injury and most likely death. We have ridden them numerous times at Walt Disney World and we thoroughly enjoy the trip along the skyways. We highly recommend you ride them if you go, but do it inside the train.

MAY THE GHOSTS BE WITH YOU

For many years, Disney has had a working relationship with Lucasfilm, with a lot of focus on the *Star Wars* franchise. They have rides and attractions based on the many films and TV shows produced by the company, as well as shops that sell *Star Wars* merchandise. Star Wars Weekend at Hollywood Studios in Disney World was an enormous success for many years, running in 1997, 2001-2002, and then 2004-2015. The event ended due to the upcoming *Star Wars*: Galaxy's Edge area that will open at Disneyland Park in Disneyland and Hollywood Studios in Walt Disney World in 2019.

Disney officially purchased Lucasfilm and all its properties and copyrights in 2012. One reason was obviously due to the massive earning potential the company and all its franchises brings. Another reason was to help Disney establish a relationship with male audiences. Over the years, Disney has excelled in reaching a female audience with their Disney Princesses, but they hadn't really caught the attention of male moviegoers, with the exception of Pixar's *Cars.* The acquisition of *Star Wars,* as well as the Marvel Universe, has opened up that avenue. Disney has launched new films, merchandise, media, and an attraction centered on the Star Wars brand and intends to continue this trend.

One of Disneyland's most renowned attractions regarding *Star Wars* was once Star Tours, a motion simulator adventure through space that took you to the planet of Endor amid attacks from the Empire. When it debuted in Disneyland in 1987, it was the first attraction based on intellectual property not owned by Disney. Its immense popularity led to 1989 openings in Tokyo Disneyland and Disney's Hollywood Studios in Walt Disney World, and then at Disneyland Park (Paris) in 1992.

From there, the ride continued to grow in popularity so much that Disney decided it needed an upgrade. In 2010, Star Tours closed in both Disneyland and Disney World to make way for a new version called Star Tours – The Adventures Continue. Tokyo closed its version in 2012 and Paris in 2016.

We rode the old Star Tours a couple of times. If you sat in the back, you got the wildest experience of the ride due to all the rising and jerking of the cabin. We have yet to ride the new version but we can only imagine how much fun it probably is.

Prior to closing, a cast member in Disneyland made a strange discovery just before the ride was about to start. There was an empty seat in cabin 2 and the worker watching the security cameras spotted something chilling in that seat. Seated there, seemingly looking up at the camera was the faint apparition of a ghostly, skeletal child. Others subsequently spotted this image as well.

Those who are skeptical of the image have claimed it is screen burn. The problem with that explanation is that the image is not always on the screen, and when it is, it's not always in the same spot.

Others have said it could be an older image showing up on reused film, except that it doesn't look entirely human. Usually when this is the case, the image will appear to be definitely human, like that of a photograph, only faint and transparent, such as the rider on Tower of Terror. While certainly looking humanoid, the image from the old Star Tours ride is misshapen and malformed. It almost looks like Casper, and it's large, curvy eyes are dark and hollow. It's hard to believe this is a previously recorded person from older film.

Of course, others have said it's a result of dust or smudges on the security cameras. It's possible that dust and smudges that get on the lenses make the same shapes repeatedly on the camera. Maybe there is some sort of shape smeared in so deeply that whenever too much dust or grime gets on the camera it makes this image. Such things have happened with windows and mirrors. They may not be the same surfaces, but it's not impossible.

Naturally, others have called this pareidolia, which is the favorite go-to explanation for the skeptic. While we certainly believe pareidolia can explain many images thought to be ghosts, we believe it's hard to attribute this explanation to more distinct images. Pareidolia better describes images such as the Man in the

Moon, Elephant Rock, and shapes appearing in clouds. Those images are clearly a result of pareidolia. The paranormal is different, especially with a picture such as the boy on Star Tours, which is much harder to call pareidolia and then say, "case closed". The boy on Star Tours is very distinct and hard to explain away as pareidolia. That's not to say that it isn't pareidolia, it's just not as likely.

We think there is a more likely explanation that pareidolia or stains on the lens, however. If there is an explanation that is not paranormal, then it's probably that the image is a reflection coming from the ride. It might be a reflection of Capt. Rex, the robot that hosted the ride. It's possible it could be C-3PO, who also made an appearance. If you take a close look at the image, it certainly seems possible. The numerous flashes of light and rockiness of the cabin could explain why the image appeared in different spots.

Or maybe it really is a spirit of someone who loved the ride. You can look at a picture of the image at strangerdimensions.com in an article called "The Ghosts That Rides Star Tours."

One reason to believe it could possibly be some paranormal manifestation is the report that another area nearby is haunted. After you left Star Tours, you would enter the *Star Wars* gift shop called the Star Trader, which some believe to be haunted.

Many cast members who have worked there say that the stock room on the fourth floor has a very heavy and depressing atmosphere. Employees who go in there have sometimes experienced sudden feelings of immense dread and anxiety. Others have described the feeling of being watched while in the room. People heard unidentified bumps and noises in the room, as well. Items on shelves and in the floor sometimes move to other locations overnight despite employees locking the room at close. I guess you could say they have a bad feeling about being in there.

Is it possible that the spirit of a child drifts around the area that was once home to Star Tours? It seems as though some sort of energy may be around. If you ever find yourself in that room, be careful because it might be a trap.

Star Wars Weekend 2010

Not Star Wars Weekend, but near the Star Wars attractions at Hollywood Studios

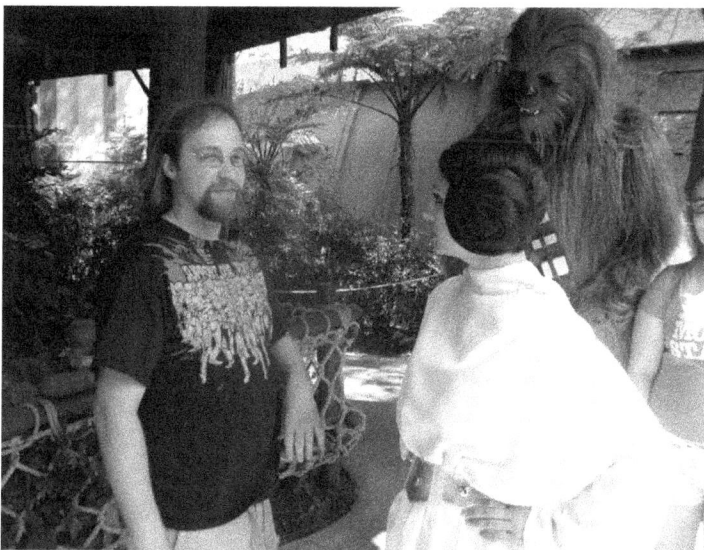

Leia was not pleased with Jacob's shirt

Jenny and the Jedi Princesses; she makes friends everywhere she goes

Hanging out near the Star Wars area of Hollywood Studios

Jenny found the Jawas

THE FRIGHTENING FLOYDS

THE GHOST IN THE STETSON

The Wilderness Lodge, located in the Magic Kingdom Resort Area in Walt Disney World, is a deluxe resort that opened in 1994. The theme is that of the national parks in the western United States. The primary architect, Peter Dominick, was an outdoorsmen and fisherman who grew up in Colorado. No doubt, he used this setting as inspiration for his design. Old Faithful Inn at Yellowstone was the inspiration for the main building. Always inspired to be authentic as they possibly can be, Disney had the Lodgepole pine that makes up the hotel's eight floors imported from Oregon. The interior design features artifacts and symbols representing mostly Northwestern Native American legends and traditions.

Most of the hotels at Disney World have some sort of cafeteria or snack area. The deluxe resorts have their own table service restaurants within. At the Wilderness Lodge, that restaurant is the Whispering Canyon Café, which possesses an Old West theme not only in food, but in the rowdy antics as well.

We've been there several times, and twice we had a waiter named "Dusty Trails" who, when coming to our table, threw our napkins in the air and let them flutter down around us. When we asked for our straws, he brought out a handful of them and tossed them on our table. On our first trip to Disney World in 2008, we ate breakfast there and when Jenny said Jacob needed ketchup, the waiter (who wasn't Dusty Trails this time), blew a whistle and started yelling for ketchup. This led to everyone in the restaurant bringing their ketchup bottles to our table and leaving them there. This, as well as Dusty Trail's behavior, was a tradition carried on at the Whispering Canyon for a number of years. In 2018 however, Disney elected to stop these antics without really giving an explanation. The rumor is that this change came about due to complaints from hotel guests. Since the restaurant is located down in the main lobby, near to many rooms, it is easy for guests to hear the commotion. Apparently, many did not like it.

Not all disturbances in the hotel come from the shenanigans taking place at the Whispering Canyon Café. There have been rumors of a ghostly man in a Stetson seen wandering the grounds. Staff and guests alike have reported seeing this ghostly image floating down the hallways and hanging around near the bathrooms by the cafe late at night after close.

One staff member said that while he was making his late-night rounds through the lodge, he experienced a sudden and drastic drop in temperature down one hall. He didn't understand why that happened, but he ignored it and went on. After walking a little further, he noticed a man with a cowboy hat on walking towards him in the distance. He noted that man was moving very fast, almost as if he was running. As the staff member drew nearer, he saw that the man was not running but floating and that he was transparent. This frightened him quite a bit.

Stetson likes to socialize with people, sometimes trying to speak to them and following them. Someone who used to work at Wilderness Lodge on third shift said Stetson used to follow him around at a distance. He would sometimes see the spirit near rooms, far down hallways, and in one of the corners of the main lobby. Another former employee claimed that Stetson said hello to her outside the women's restroom one night. Guests have apparently told stories about approached by the ghostly cowboy, as well.

During a stretch of a couple weeks, the club level lounge received repeated phone calls from a room that was out of inventory. When staff members investigated it, they found no sign that anyone had been staying in the room. Furthermore, the phone cord was no longer in the jack, which is weird in itself.

We stayed at Wilderness Lodge twice and visit there every time we take a trip to Disney World. We've never encountered Stetson. Hopefully we will next time we're there. We did have a strange occurrence while staying there. Late in the night, around 3am, we woke to the sound of a robotic voice yelling in the hall. At first, we couldn't determine what was happening. Then we realized that it was accompanied by an alarm, and the voice was telling us to get out. We then realized we were hearing the fire alarm.

Once the hotel evacuation was completed, the fire department came. After the fiasco was over, we asked around about what was going on. There had been no fire and no one had called the fire department. As far as they could find out, no one had pulled any of the alarms. What had caused this major disturbance was a complete mystery to the hotel staff, who we questioned that night and the following day. Not that we expect staff members would tells us what was happening anyway.

Could this have been Stetson trying to rile everyone up, or was it a simple slip in the lodge's technology? Maybe seeing the hootenannies that used to take place at the café gave him some ideas. We guess we'll never know.

Another memorable experience we had came during out most recent trip in January of 2019. Though our favorite hotel to stay at is the French Quarter at Riverside, we make sure to visit the other hotels we like. Among those is Wilderness Lodge.

On this trip, we came to Disney World in very early January, just after Christmas and New Year's. We were hoping we would have the opportunity to see the holiday decorations around the Disney. When we arrived at the Wilderness Lodge, ate dinner at the Roaring Forks café, and looked around for a few. The Wilderness Lodge has a Christmas tree that stands about four stories, and we arrived there just in time to see it because after we took a few pictures of it, the tree movers showed up to take it down.

Apparently, it is quite the process to take down and remove this tree, which is not surprising. Its immensity is overwhelming, and a crew of what looked like twenty people or more poured in with pulleys, carts, and a moving truck to tear it down and haul it out. Before we left, one of the crew members was nice enough to take our picture near a couple of much smaller trees. It was neat to see this towering Christmas tree and what a major ordeal it is to dismantle it.

At the waterfall outside of the Wilderness Lodge

At Wilderness Lodge in early January of 2019, just after Christmas; we got there just as they were about to take down the trees. In fact, one of the members of the crew disassembling the trees took this picture.

The gargantuan Christmas tree just before they took it down. In the background, you can see a couple of the workers involved with the tree's removal.

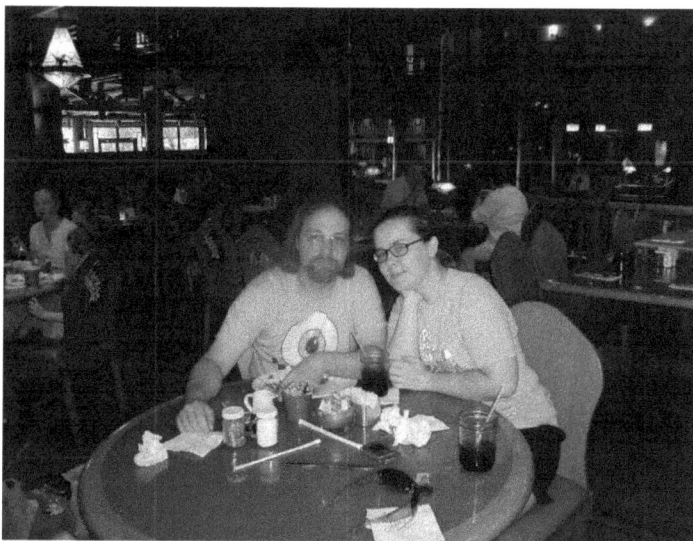

At the Whispering Canyon Café for the first time

All the ketchup bottles the patrons of the Whispering Canyon Café brought to Jacob

THE URN OF GRANDMA JOYCE

For many years now there have been tales of people scattering loved ones' ashes somewhere on Disney property. Disneyland alone has had it happen on numerous occasions, according to unofficial reports. More specifically than that, the Haunted Mansion is said to have been the recipient of a dearly departed patron's remains more than once. But as one story states, one family took this practice to the next level.

One night, the crew for Disneyland's Haunted Mansion spotted guesst dumping a powdery substance from each side of their Doom Buggy. The ride was then stopped and searched. Though they could clearly see the act taking place on security footage, the crew could not identify which buggy was responsible, so the ride continued.

Later that night at closing, one of the cast members noticed some of the plants in the spooky garden had been moved. Upon inspecting this, they found an empty urn buried a few inches in the ground. Engraved on the urn was, "Rest in Peace Our Dearest Grandma Joyce."

For several months, the urn was kept in the surveillance room of the Haunted Mansion. Finally, some of the cast members decided to do something nice for Grandma Joyce: They took her urn up on the catwalk overlooking the graveyard scene and made a memorial for her. That is the story, yet we have never had this confirmed. If this tale is indeed true, who knows if the memorial remains, but no doubt the remains are still somewhere on the ride as the cast members never found the ashes. Perhaps Grandma Joyce remains as well.

BE OUR GHOST

PETER PAN'S FRIGHT

Peter Pan's Flight is one of Disneyland's original rides. It opened in July of 1955, not long after the park opened. The Walt Disney World version opened in 1971, expanding on the California ride's original concept. It is a dark ride that has you in a rail-suspended car about seventeen feet off the ground, flying over a makeshift London. The attraction uses forced perspective to make it seem like you are actually higher than that. The original intention of the ride was to put you in the magical shoes of Peter Pan as he makes his nightly flights with the Lost Boys. This confused guests, however, since the attraction did not feature Peter Pan. The ride in Walt Disney World does feature Pan.

We rode this ride during our first trip to Disney World in 2008 and really enjoyed it. Each time we returned, we always wanted to ride it but were unable to for one reason or another. It wasn't until our summer trip in 2018 that we were able to join Pan and company on their flight once again. A decade later, we enjoyed the ride every bit as much.

We're not the only couple that loves Peter Pan's Flight. Cast members have reported sightings of a spectral couple that looks forward to taking flight. The man is tall and bald and the woman has long hair. They are often seen standing at the end of the line late at night when there aren't many people waiting. One cast member said he was working the ride and saw them standing down there three or four times throughout the evening but never saw them board. Another reported seeing them at the end of the line three different days, several weeks apart.

As far as we know, no guests have ever reported seeing the couple. Not that this is surprising. They are most likely seen as just another couple in line, and since they don't seem to bother anyone, they wouldn't be making themselves known.

THE FRIGHTENING FLOYDS

Peter Pan's Flight is one of the busiest rides in all of Disney and usually has some of the longest wait times. We highly recommend you ride it, but get a Fast Pass for it or you might end up like the ghostly couple waiting in line for years.

And we thought we waited a long time to ride that ride again.

After riding Peter Pan's Flight for the first time in 2008

THE FRIGHTENING FLOYDS

THE MAN WITH NO EYES

One of the most popular attractions at Disney World's Animal Kingdom is Dinosaur, located in DinoLand U.S.A. Formerly known as Countdown to Extinction, the ride opened with Animal Kingdom on April 22nd, 1998. To promote the 2000 animated film, *Dinosaur*, Disney changed the name of the attraction. It is a dark ride with an enhanced motion vehicle (theme park technology invented by Disney) with many dinosaur animatronics. The rider is sent back to the Cretaceous period, just before the catastrophic asteroid strike, by a scientist to capture an Iguanodon. Along the way, a Carnotaurus pursues you. It's a lot of fun and we have ridden it a couple of times.

Lucky for us we never sat next to the man alleged to haunt the ride. Riders have reported sitting next to a stoic, unmoving elderly man who does not acknowledge them when they speak to him. In fact, he does not react at all to anything around him. Witnesses say he sits still, staring ahead, not screaming, not speaking, and not even blinking. When the ride is over, he doesn't even get out behind them.

To make matters even more curious, he often doesn't show up in pictures. As with most of Disney's dark rides, there is a moment just before a scare or a big drop when your picture is taken in hopes of catching you in the middle of screaming or reacting somehow to what is about to happen. It seems that many times whenever guests who have sat with this creepy man check their photos, he isn't there. Not every time, though. On a few occasions, the man has shown up in pictures. But when he does, it's even creepier than when he doesn't because he has no eyes.

If you fail to bring back the Iguanodon, maybe you'll bring back this interesting individual instead.

At Animal Kingdom, 2009

There we are in the back. Thankfully, everyone in the picture has eyes.

ABANDONED RIVER COUNTRY

Outside of the four main parks at Walt Disney World (Magic Kingdom, Epcot, Hollywood Studio, and Animal Kingdom), there are also the two water parks—Typhoon Lagoon and Blizzard Beach. Both offer a lot of water fun if you want to spend a day cooling off from the heated bustle of the other locations. Typhoon Lagoon opened in 1989 and Blizzard Beach in 1995. Neither of these are the first water park, however. That distinction belongs to the park that opened in 1976 known as River Country.

River Country was located on the Shore of Bay Lake near Discovery Island, another abandoned Disney attraction. This rustic-style theme park resembled an old-fashioned swimming hole consisting of two pools and five water slides. Initially, it was to be named Pop's Willow Grove—and we can't help but think that not going with this name was probably a good decision—and was inspired by *The Adventures of Huckleberry Finn.*

The park did pretty well, but Typhoon Lagoon was larger, had better parking, and more slides, so it took a lot of attention away from River Country after it opened in '89. When Blizzard Beach opened in '95, it took even more attention from River Country as it was much larger, too. When River Country closed at the end of warm-weather season on November 2nd, 2001, it was expected that it would reopen as usual in spring of '02. However, the April 11th, 2002 edition of the *Orlando Sentinel* reported that River Country might not reopen, to which Disney responded that it would reopen if there were enough customer demand. In 2005, Disney officially announced that River Country would not reopen and it has sat abandoned ever since.

Though there has not been anything ghostly occurring there, it is quite fascinating that Disney has allowed an inactive park to rot away for more than ten years. It might not be paranormal, but some find this to be odd.

A photographer who goes by the assumed name of Seph Lawless broke into the vacated park in 2016 and snapped some eerie photos of the decay that had taken place there over the fifteen years between its closing and his trespassing. In his photo collection, you see that branches, bramble, and vines have overtaken bridges. Weeds and high grass now cover roads and pathways. The intricate and elaborate rides now stand lonely against the horizon. Trees have grown up around the pools, dumping dead leaves, moss, and other debris into the murky, stagnant water. Broken pieces of attractions and buildings lay scattered about, and some parts of rides even engulfed by the thriving plant life. Trees block slides that have become dirty and twisted by the branches growing around them. Smudgy deflated rafts still float in Bay Cove, one of the park's main attractions. Offices looked like they were hurriedly abandoned, and the filthy furniture, paperwork, and various items remain scattered all over the rooms. Some of the park is still visible from Bay Lake.

When Disney caught Lawless, they banned him for life from Disney World immediately. This has led others to speculate that Disney is trying to cover something up. What that could be, who knows? There were three deaths that happened at River Country: two drownings (1982 and 1989) and an eleven-year-old boy who died of a brain infection known as amoebic meningoencephalitis in August 1980; it was concluded that this disease came from an amoeba in the waters at River Country. It's hard to believe that's what Disney is covering up since these cases are public knowledge. They could have just banned Lawless for trespassing in a closed-off and dangerous location. You know, being in Florida, that abandoned park likely has alligators, snakes, and other dangerous wildlife living in it.

They also intend to build a lakeside resort over the vacated park called Reflections – A Disney Lakeside Lodge. Any sort of bad press or lawsuit over someone injured by fallen debris or killed by a wild animal could certainly hinder a project like that. It's easy to imagine why Disney would not want anyone in there and why they would ban someone who violates their rule. Of course, we never rule out any possibilities for secret operations transpiring somewhere.

Besides, what could they be hiding at the abandoned theme parks? If they really wanted to do anything shadowy and illicit, they'd just use Club 33. Isn't that right?

THE FRIGHTENING FLOYDS

THE GHOSTS OF TOM SAWYER ISLAND

Surrounded by the Rivers of America, Disneyland's Tom Sawyer Island is one of the park's remaining original attractions. In 2007, it underwent renovations that saw the addition of Pirate's Lair, which includes references to the *Pirates of the Caribbean* films. This was done in an attempt to add some freshness to the attraction. Tom Sawyer Island closed in 2016, but reopened the following year.

In 1973, an 18-year-old man by the name of Bogden Delaurot and his ten-year-old brother hid out on Tom Sawyer Island until the park closed. According to the story, Bogden's brother could not swim, so he put his little brother on his back and started swimming across the Rivers of America. The plan was for the boys to play in the park after dark. However, Bogden did not make it; he drowned trying to convey his brother to safety. The little boy lived.

Bogden's drowning is not the only tragedy to have happened around Tom Sawyer Island. In 1983, a drunken man by the name of Philip Straughan drowned near the Island while attempting to swim through the Rivers of America.

These deaths we read about through blogs and articles online but have never seen any official reports. While we believe them to be true, and are almost certain they are, we cannot say with absolution.

According to sources, the spirit of the brother who drowned has been seen swimming across the water. Some tales tell that both boys drowned and thus both have been seen there in spirit form. Others claim that their calls for help can be heard at night. Also, the sounds of children playing on the island have been heard when no children were there. Some believe this to be the spirits of children who have passed but once played there returning to a fond memory in the afterlife.

BE OUR GHOST

THE FRIGHTENING FLOYDS

WALT STILL AT DISNEY

We have explored the reports that Walt Disney still haunts Disneyland in our previous book, *Haunts of Hollywood Stars and Starlets,* in which we also discussed Disney's rise to fame. Undoubtedly, Walt Disney is one of the most important names in the entertainment world. The Chicago native persevered through many failures and misfortunes to build one of the biggest media empires the world has ever known. He has won 26 Academy Awards and is considered one of the greatest pioneers in animation. His parks attract millions of people around the world each year. Now, with the recent acquisitions of Lucasfilm, Marvel Studios, 20th Century Fox, and Fox Searchlight, it seems there's no stopping the Walt Disney Company.

The same can be said for Walt himself. Despite his death, nothing seems to be able to stop him from visiting his beloved park. There are reports that he haunts a few different areas around Disneyland.

Walt had an apartment above the fire station on Main Street, U.S.A. in Disneyland. Whenever he stayed there, he kept a light burning in the window to let workers know he was there. After his death, the staff wished to leave the room just as Walt had left it, with only minimal tidying up. Rumor has it that the apartment is almost exactly how it was when Walt passed, with even the papers he was working on still lying on his desk. We're not sure if that part of the story is true however, because when researching about the apartment, we found that it has been restored to the exact state it was in when the park first opened in 1955, and that tours of the apartment are available. We have not seen the apartment for ourselves so we are not sure which version of the story is true.

However, there is a story about a cleaning lady who had an encounter with the ghost of Walt Disney. Not long after he died, the cleaning lady was touching up the room a bit and when she was done, she turned off the light in the window. When she got back outside, she looked up and saw that the light was back on. Thinking that maybe she had neglected to turn it off all the way, she went back in and made sure to extinguish it completely. Again, when she got back out to the street, she saw that someone had relit the lamp.

Now concerned that someone was in there, she went back in and looked around, finding no one present. She then turned the light off again and stayed in the room to see if it came back on. A few seconds later, it did. Then she heard a voice whisper, "I'm still here." She left the apartment and never went back inside. Now, people supposedly only enter the apartment to relight the lamp when it has burned out.

There is one version of the story that we reported in *Haunts of Hollywood* that stated the cleaning lady had unplugged the lamp but it came back on, and she then saw someone pull back the curtains in the room and look out at her. While it's very possible that the curtain portion of this story is true, we doubt seriously that she pulled the plug on the lamp since the lamp is not electric. We have never been to Disneyland to see the lamp for ourselves and we had just learned this recently. Misinformation is sometimes the issue when reporting urban legends and ghost tales, and we usually go the extra mile to ensure we have the story right. Unfortunately, this would seem to have been an oversight on our end.

Employees who have gone into the room to relight the lamp have heard loud knocks on the walls and footsteps moving across the room. Some who have been down in the firehouse below have reported hearing bangs, knocks, and footsteps coming from the apartment above them.

A well-respected psychic medium named Michael Kouri released a book called *The Ghost of Walt Disney & Me* chronicling his time spent in the apartment with the likes of Roy Disney and author Ray Bradbury. While there, Kouri reports strange and frightening occurrences began, such as the toilet flushing, faucets running, strange sounds in the cupboards, and even phantom phone calls with nothing more than static on the other end.

In 2009, a Disneyland security camera caught the transparent image of a man walking out of the Haunted Mansion and through the park long after it had closed. He walked through fences and across water. Since the video surfaced on YouTube, it has led to many debates about the nature of it. Some say it's an image from old footage bleeding over, but others seem to think it's the ghost of Walt Disney taking a stroll through his beloved park. Those who believe it's a ghost ask why it was only one man's image burned into the footage. They also ask why he was moving so quickly through the park. These are both interesting questions to consider. Personally, we think it's odd that the person's entire walk was burned into the footage. Was the image metaphysical or just a simple malfunction in technology?

The area above the Pirates of the Caribbean ride in Disneyland allegedly houses the spirit of Walt, as well as his wife Lillian. At one time, this was the Disney Gallery, an exhibition of artwork from Walt Disney Imagineering. For 20 years, from 1987 to 2007, it was located in the area above POTC in New Orleans Square. The Gallery has since moved, but during the two decades it was there, people had reported seeing Walt and Lillian Disney walking around the Formal Sitting Room, enjoying the artwork. They had also been seen in the Collector's Room, sitting down as if relaxing after a long day. Walt often stood in the vestibule by himself, as if waiting for Lillian. Lillian lingered on the balcony and patio after close.

Some believe Walt likes to watch the firework display brighten the night sky over Sleeping Beauty Castle. There is a forty-second video on YouTube that shows the end of the show and some think this video captured the image of Walt Disney's ghost standing on the castle, looking up at the fireworks. If you look closely at the image in the video, you can see that it is most certainly the image of a person. It's not smoke making the shape of a human as tt remains in place, not drifting as smoke does. It looks like a back shot of the Partners statue, where Walt is holding Mickey Mouse's hand and pointing. There is a Partners in Disney World and in front of Sleeping Beauty Castle, but there is no such statue actually *on* Sleeping Beauty Castle. What's more, once the firework show ends, the figure looks as if it turns around and begins walking, only to fade away.

It is a very interesting video. We watched several more videos and looked at numerous pictures of the Disneyland firework show, and never saw the image again. Now, could it have been some holographic image of Walt? Maybe so. Disney likes to slide in hidden gems like that into their shows, movies, and attractions all the time. Only it seems there would be other videos with the shot in it.

This reminds us of a story we read while researching Walt's apartment on Main Street. On Disneyland's opening day, the Mouseketeers were in Walt's apartment with him watching everyone come in. One Mouseketeer said that when all the people came pouring in, Walt stood there with his hands behind his back, tears in his eyes, and a grin on his face. The mysterious image on top of Sleeping Beauty Castle is reminiscent of that description.

We can't say if that shape captured on video was truly the ghost of Walt Disney, or a ghost at all, but it certainly is interesting to look at. Perhaps he is still standing in Disneyland, watching the wonders that have come out of it since his death, still smiling at the colossal achievement. If it's true that Walt's spirit remains at Disneyland, we're also glad to hear Lillian is with him. Nothing better than sharing eternity with your dream and the person you loved most in the world.

AFTERWORD: SEE YOU REAL SOON

We hope you enjoyed the fascinating ghost stories and other stories from the Disney Parks. Whether or not one is a believer in the paranormal, it's always fun to play ghost. For those who are believers, it's always fun to hear more supernatural stories, especially from somewhere as famous as is Disney.

Though we had no definitive ghostly experiences ourselves at Disney World, we would like to share one of our favorite memories in closing.

It happened in August of 2018, just a few months back from the writing of this chapter. Every time we go to Disney World we are early risers. We like to be at the park gates when they open because that gives you early access to rides before the major crowds come pouring in. On the other hand, we also despise hot weather, but we used to tough it out anyway. During our 2018 trip, we decided to show up early, get half the park done, then go back to the hotel, take a nap, and go back to the park when the sun was going down. Not only is it much cooler during these hours, most of the families have left the parks, leaving smaller groups, smaller crowds, and shorter lines. This actually made the trip more fun, not just because wait times were down and the weather was cooler, but also because we are night people by nature.

What also makes the strategy sound when going to Magic Kingdom is that if you time it right, you can arrive during the fireworks show, which distracts people from the other attractions. We had already seen fireworks display numerous times. When we stayed at Wilderness Lodge, we heard and saw the show every night since the Magic Kingdom is very close. Though this was a different show than it was back then, we decided we'd rather go back to the Haunted Mansion ride for the second time that day. This was the same day Jacob neglected to tell George, "Good morning." The Haunted Mansion broke down when we rode it the second time, too.

The memory that we really loved about it was as we were dashing through the park, passing the crowds of people watching the show, the fireworks were exploding in the sky, thundering, flashing in the night sky, and lighting the park in numerous colors all around us while the show's music played. It was a lot of fun, especially since it really felt like it was just us as we were the only people heading for the rides.

Once again, thanks for reading. This time around, we were glad to be able to write a book with a personal touch. While we are often able to put at least something personal into our paranormal books, *Louisville's Strange and Unusual Haunts* was the only one with mostly firsthand experiences. Though we witnessed none of these Disney paranormal reports, we were able to speak with some people who had, and having been to Disney World a few times helps give us at least a little perspective on some of the tales. We were glad to be able to share some of that with our readers because you have all been so supportive and we appreciate every bit of it.

Ahead are some photos taken while we were at Disney World. We hope you enjoy.

Until next time, thanks for reading. See you real soon!

THE FRIGHTENING FLOYDS

THE FRIGHTENING FLOYDS' DISNEY GALLERY

Ahead are some pictures of our time spent at Walt Disney World in Orlando, FL. It's a special place to us because when we first got together, even though we had virtually nothing at all, we managed to save up for a trip with our meager salaries. As we've worked to improve things over the years, we have always had new experiences at Disney. As we have grown, so have the memories. This is not even really the tip of the iceberg, but a few of our experiences captured forever. We intend for there to be many more.

Thank you for taking the time to come on the trip with us.

Posing with the gators at our favorite resort, Port Orleans French Quarter

Enjoying the atmosphere of the French Quarter

Visiting other resorts is something we like to do. This is Pride Rock at the Art of Animation.

Hakuna Matata

Under the Sea!

The Art of Animation has separate areas themed to different Disney films

Who doesn't love *The Little Mermaid*?

Halloween at Magic Kingdom

October is also Jacob's birth month, so visiting Disney around Halloween was extra special for us.

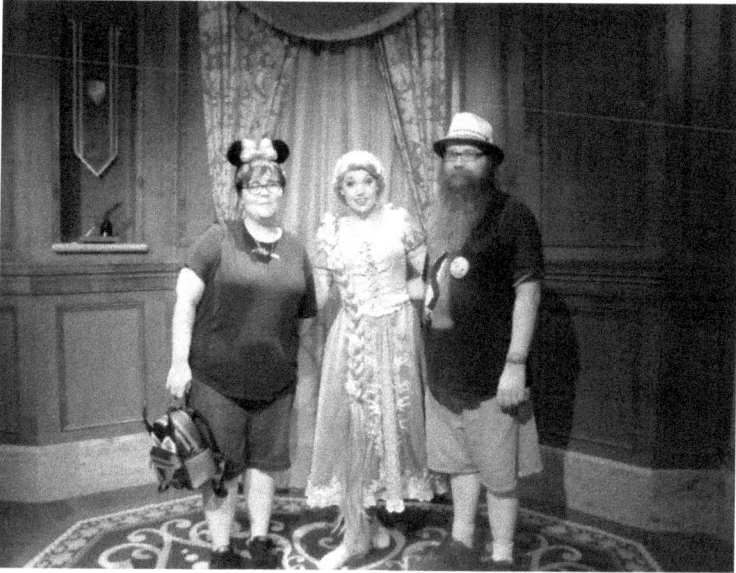

Disney Memory: Rapunzel calling Jacob a ruffian and asking Jenny if he was bothering her. LOL

Chilling at the Magic Kingdom after dark

This time on Splash Mountain, Jacob pointed out the camera to everyone. Strike a pose!

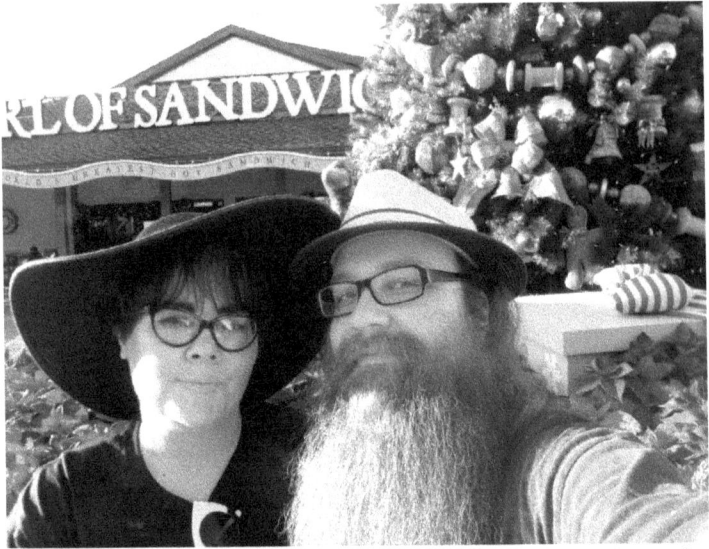

Sitting by a Christmas tree outside the Earl of Sandwich at Disney Springs

Enjoying some shopping and sightseeing at Disney Springs; Jacob even picked up a new Bowler for his hat collection

We were finally able to meet a mermaid. Ariel really liked Jenny's sunglasses.

ABOUT THE AUTHORS

Jacob and Jenny Floyd are the Frightening Floyds – paranormal authors, publishers, ghost tour operators, and Disney enthusiasts. They currently live in Louisville, KY with their three dogs (Tarzan, Pegasus, and Snow White, aka BooBoo) and three cats (Baloo, Narnia, and Pandora Opossum, otherwise known as Pandy Possum). They hope to one day move to Orlando, for obvious reasons. You can follow their work on Facebook, Twitter, and Instagram.

BIBLIOGRAPHY

Disneyworld.com

"George, the Ghost of Walt Disney World's Pirates of the Caribbean" by Rob Schwarz at strangerdimensions.com

"WDW Myth: Pirates of the Caribbean is Being Haunted" by George at forums.wdwmagic.com

"Are There Real Skeletons in Disneyland's Pirates of the Caribbean?" At mentalfloss.com

"Real Human Skulls in Pirates of the Caribbean Disneyland" by Gavin Doyle at disneydose.com

"6 Spooky Myths About Ghosts That Haunt Disney's Theme Parks" by Nick Sim at themeparktourist.com

"Haunted Disneyland: Ghosts in the Happiest Place on Earth" at wanderwisdom.com

"9 Ghosts That Reportedly Haunts Disney Parks, From Urban Legends to Actual Events in the Park's History" by Lucia Peters at bustle.com

"Living and Dying in the Magic Kingdom: The Ghosts of Disneyland" at legacysunfoldingjourney.blogspot.com

"Disco Debbie Still Grooving at Space Mountain" at ifunny.co

"The Ghosts of Disneyland and Other Creepy Disney Legends" by Alyse Wax at the13thfloor.tv

"Haunted Disneyland: Ghosts in the Happiest Place on Earth" at wanderwisdom.com

"Disneyland – The Creepiest Place on Earth" at backpackerverse.com

"9 Creepy Disney Park Legends You Should Know Before Planning Your Next Trip" at viralnova.com

"Frightening Facts about the Twilight Zone Tower of Terror" at disneyworldenthusiast.com

"Disney Ghosts Stories: The Ghostly Bellhop on Tower of Terror" at doctordisney.com

"13 Freaky Facts about Disney's Tower of Terror Ride" by Stacy Conradt at mentalfloss.com

"10 Scary, Legendary Ghost Tales of Disneyland Haunts" by Keith Sharon at ocregister.com

"Disney World Ghosts Stories" at disneyworldenthusiast.com

"12 Urban Legends about Tokyo Disneyland" at soranews24.com

"Johnny Depp as Jack Sparrow Makes Surprise Appearance at Pirates of the Caribbean Disneyland Ride" by Nellie Andreeva at deadline.com

"Thirteen Fun Facts about the Haunted Mansion" at d23.com

"Weird and Wonderful Haunted Mansion Facts, Secrets, and History" by Arthur Levine at tripsavvy.com

"To Tell the Truth: The Ballroom Spider in Disneyland's Haunted Mansion" by Makena Wolcott at wdwradio.com

"20 Scary Facts about the Haunted Mansion at Disneyland" by Chris Dallin at getawaytoday.com

"The Feral Cats of Disneyland" by Kyle Jaeger at vice.com

"The Cats of Disneyland" at disneylandcats.com

Disneylandclub33.com

"Peek Inside Disney's Secretive Club 33" at ripleys.com

"The Wilderness Lodge is Haunted" at disboards.com

"Folklore of Disney's Fort Wilderness and Bay Lake: Myth of Reality" at wildernessprincess.net

"The History of Disney's Wilderness Lodge – Part One" by Chuck Mirarchi at wdwinfo.com

"Star Wars: Why Disney was Destined to Buy Lucasfilm" by James Russell at theguardian.com

"The Ghost that Rides Star Tours" by Rob Schwarz at strangerdimensions.com

"17 Disney Park Conspiracy Theories That'll Scare the Hell Out of You" by Anna Kopsky at buzzfeed.com

"Haunted Mansion Cursed Table?" at magicqueenstar.tumblr.com

"Creepy Stories and Legends about Disneyland" by Lisa Waugh at ranker.com

"Happy Haunts: 15 of the Creepiest Real-life Stories from Disney Parks" by Robin Burks at thethings.com

"Dark Side of Disneyland: 10 Ghost Stories and Urban Legends" at theoccultmuseum.com

"17 Horror Stories That'll Change the Way You See Disney World" by Travis Furman at onedio.co

"15 Disney Locations That Are Haunted (And the Creepy Stories Behind Them)" by Ossiana Tepfenhart at therichest.com

"The Heartbreaking True Story Behind the Rumors of a Matterhorn Ghost" by Jessica Leigh Mattern at countryliving.com

"Ghosts at Disney World" at tripadvisor.com

"Disneyland: The Happiest Haunted Place on Earth" at echoesofthesouthwest.com

Teendisney.com

"A Tribute to Walt Disney World's River Country" at bigfloridacountry.com

"River Country Closed by Brain-Eating Amoeba" at yesterland.com

"As Crowds Dry Up, Disney Closes River Country Park" published April 11th, 2002 by the *Orlando Sentinel*, and can be found at orlandosentinel.com

"Abandoned: The Rise, Fall and Decay of Disney's River Country" by Nick Sim at themeparktourist.com

"What Happened to River Country? Inside Disney's Creepiest Theme Park" by Gavin Fernando at news.com.au

"This Abadoned Disney Water Park has Been Rotting for Over 15 Years – Now it's Turning into a Resort" by Leanna Garfield at businessinsider.com

"8 Facts and Secrets about Peter Pan's Flight at Disney's Magic Kingdom Park" by Christy Caby at disneylists.com

"Walt Disney Still at the Happiest Place on Earth" from *Haunts of Hollywood Stars and Starlets* by the Frightening Floyds

"Take a Tour of Walt Disney's Secret Disneyland Apartment" at maps.roadtrippers.com

"Tokyo Disneyland – Cinderella's Fairy Tale Hall" at dejiki.com

"*Happily Ever After* Nighttime Spectacular will Debut at Magic Kingdom Park May 12th" by Jennifer Fickley-Baker at disneyparks.disney.go.com

"Cinderella's Castle" at disneyworld.disney.go

"The Unique Histories of 6 Disney Icons" by Kevin Siruss at themeparktourist.com

"Cinderella's Royal Table" at Disneyworld.disney.go

"Park Secrets Disney Doesn't Want You to Know Gallery" by Carolyn Menyes at thedailymeal.com

"Ghosts Watches Fireworks from Disneyland Castle" uploaded by Danloganify on YouTube.com

"5 Horrible "Deaths" at Disney Theme Parks (That Never Really Happened)" by Nick Sim at themeparktourist.com

"13 Stories Down: On the Anniversary of *The Twilight Zone* Tower of Terror" at ohmy.disney.com

"Top 5 Walt Disney World Resorts at Christmas Time" by Liliane Opsomer at smallworldvacations.com

"Disneyland's Most Famous Deaths" by Simone Haruko Smith at wanderwisdom.com

"Tom Sawyer Island: Haunted Disneyland!" by Scott Markus and Connor Bright at voicesfromthegrave.wordpress.com

"Haunted Mansion Cast Members Built a Shrine to 'Grandma Joyce' Whose Urn was Found in the Gardens" by Cory Doctorow at boingboing.net

Thank you for reading! If you like the book, please leave a review on Amazon and Goodreads. Even if you don't like it, please still leave a review.

To keep up with more Nightmare Press news, join the Anubis Press Dynasty on Facebook.

.

www.ingramcontent.com/pod-product-compliance
Lightning Source LLC
Chambersburg PA
CBHW070811050426
42452CB00011B/1987